THEPAIN FROM HER WOMB

NATASHA CATO

authorHOUSE®

AuthorHouse™
1663 Liberty Drive
Bloomington, IN 47403
www.authorhouse.com
Phone: 1 (800) 839-8640

Published by AuthorHouse 06/17/2020

ISBN: 978-1-7283-3598-8 (sc)
ISBN: 978-1-7283-3597-1 (e)

Library of Congress Control Number: 2019918695

Print information available on the last page.

Any people depicted in stock imagery provided by Getty Images are models, and such images are being used for illustrative purposes only. Certain stock imagery © Getty Images.

This book is printed on acid-free paper.

This book is dedicated to my grandmother, the late Willie Mae Cato. I miss and love you so much. Thank you for all of your love and support. Thank you for always being there for me. Thank you for your faithfulness and commitment to the Lord. Thank you for pushing me in the great direction that changed my life forever. I love you. Always continue to rest in the Lord!

I also dedicate this to my sister, the late Dalvis Small White. You taught me to always follow my dreams and my heart's desire. Thank you for all of your encouragement. I love you always. Continue to rest in the Lord.

Acknowledgments

To my pastor, Joseph I. Thomas Jr., spiritual father of Greater Blessed Hope Church of God in Christ. Thank you for being the true man of God that you are, for your faithfulness and commitment to God, ministered to many. May God continue to use you for his glory!

To my sister and prayer partner, Minister Kenya Hebert. Thank you for all of your encouraging words, your support, and your countless hours in prayer with me and for me. Thank you for pushing me and picking me up, no matter the trials and tribulations I had to face. You were always there, especially for my children. We love you! I pray that the Lord will grant you everything your heart desires. Your reward is coming. Thank you for being a faithful sister and friend. You rock!

Special thanks to my sons: Nashawn, Dane'e, Elijah, and Elisha. You guys are my pride and joy—the ones who keep me going and the ones I live for and will never stop fighting for. I love you guys with all of my heart.

To my grandchildren: Amir, Danasia, King, and Kameron. G-mom loves you!

To my mother, Carol. Thank you for the life you have given me. Thank you for all of your support through the years. I love you!

To my sister and brother, Marisa and Maurice. I love you guys so much. Thank you for always being there for me!

If I have failed to mention anyone in my acknowledgments, please know that I truly love each and every one of you who has shown encouragement to me by word, thought, and deed as I wrote this book. God bless you all.

Chapter 1

This is the story of Natasha Cato growing up in Brooklyn, New York, in a project called Eleanor Roosevelt Housing. I lived there with my grandmother, mother, brother, aunt, and uncle.

I experienced so much and saw so much as a child there. Roosevelt was one of the worst projects in Bedford-Stuyvesant. Killings, drugs, and any trouble you can name were all normal for anyone who lived or was brought up there, so it became easy for me to adapt to life's tragedies. Bed-Stuy became a part of me.

And yet I can remember from earliest childhood my grandmother taking my brother and me to church every Sunday. Grandma Willie Mae Cato was a strong believer in Christ. She was a faithful member and one of the mothers of Bright Light Church of God in Christ, and if you lived in Grandma's house, you had to go to church. That topic was not up for discussion at all—we didn't have a choice in the matter.

I remember kicking and screaming every Sunday morning because I didn't want to go to church. I wanted to stay home and play outside with my friends.

One Sunday morning, Grandma got us up for church as usual. We all got dressed, and she told me to put on my white tights. Oh, man! For the life of me, I didn't want to wear those white tights, but again, I had no choice. I put on those white tights.

As we were walking out of the house, we saw that the elevators were broken. I thought, *Good, now Grandma will change her mind about going to church.* Well, I thought wrong. Grandma headed for the door to the stairs, pausing to look at us. "Let's go!" she said.

"Oh, boy!" I mumbled under my breath. As we were walking down the stairs, I got the idea that I would pretend to fall and rip those white tights, thinking I would get to stay home. *Here I go!*

My plan appeared to have worked. There was a huge dirty hole in one knee of my little white tights. But then Grandma turned around, looked down at me there on the landing, and said, "Get up! You're going to church just like that!"

I looked up at her with tears in my eyes as if to say, *Grandma, how can you do this to me?* I tell you, I could not pull anything on Grandma—she was on point! I went to church just like that, with a big dirty hole in the knee of my little white tights. I promise you, I never did that again.

Grandma had us in church Sunday after Sunday. Rain,

sleet, or snow, we were there! We got to church before Sunday school started. We went upstairs for breakfast, and after that was morning service, followed by lunch. After lunch, we attended afternoon services. Church for us was a second home.

Growing up in church while exposed to the vicious lifestyle around me, I was torn between two worlds. I learned the things of the church as a child, with my grandmother teaching me the way to live from the Bible's perspective. Grandma was always praying for me and anointing my head with oil. Her heart's desire was to make sure that I knew God was real and the church was my safe haven—a place I could go for help.

My grandmother and my mother worked in a group home, where they were required to put in extremely long hours. Some days they would work the overnight shift. My mother, working so hard to support her children, decided she needed someone to care for me and my brother while she went to work, so she hired someone.

The person who took care of us was an elderly woman. She had her grandchildren living in her home as well, but they were much older than I was. She had us on a daily routine, and in the beginning, I was comfortable—no problems other than I just didn't want to be there.

My mother would drop us off and pick us up after her shift was over. Our elderly caretaker was very nice—she fed us healthy meals while we were there, took us out to play, and always made sure we took naps.

But as time went on, staying there for countless hours became a nightmare for me. I took my naps in a small room alone while the elderly woman sat in her bedroom watching

TV. One day, as I was taking a nap, just as I would any other day, I woke up to the sound of the front door opening. The bedroom where I took my naps was just a few steps away from the front door, so I lifted my head and looked to see who was coming in. It was the elderly woman's grandson.

He walked toward the room where I was napping and peeked in. Then he slowly approached the bed and started touching me in inappropriate places. Before I knew it, my panties were down. He ejaculated, and as he looked at me with an angry face, he whispered, "I will get you if you tell anyone!"

I was so scared at that moment. When, as always, my mother picked me up after her shift and took me home, I said nothing about what had happened, remembering what he said. I was too afraid.

He didn't stop there. It continued. Once, my mom had an overnight shift, and we stayed over until the next morning. I was in the same room where I took my naps, and there I was confronted not just by him but his sister as well.

As always, their grandmother was asleep in her bedroom. So they took me from of the bed where I was sleeping into the kitchen, which was in the back of the house. They pushed my back against the wall and had their way with me, and like the times before, I was told to never say a word.

I never did say a word to my mother about the violations I went through in that house. After a while, my mother decided for whatever reason to change our babysitter, and that chapter of my life was over.

Chapter 2

The years went by, and as I grew older, I still went to church with my grandmother—and still hung out in the projects. When I reached a certain age, I began to stray from the church, only going every once in a while. Being that I had been forced into the church as a child, I decided to go my own way. My heart was with hanging out with my friends in the projects.

By the age of fourteen or fifteen, I had developed some bad habits, including sneaking out to house parties and concerts. I began to drink and smoke weed to the point where it didn't even get me high anymore. My grandmother and mother had no idea what I had gotten myself into.

The projects I grew up in had it all, just like any other project—fighting, drugs, homicide. I found myself getting into things that a young girl shouldn't. I was hanging out and sneaking behind my grandmother's back. The trouble grew to the point where I was selling crack out of my grandmother's house, boosting and selling clothes, scamming credit cards, fighting, robbing girls at gunpoint for their earrings, and getting locked up. At the same time, Grandma was going strong as a faithful member of the church. She was going one way, and I was going another.

And then, at the age of fifteen, I became pregnant. I wanted my baby with all of my heart. I ran around in the projects hiding my pregnancy from my mother and grandmother until I couldn't anymore. When I started showing, my mother finally noticed, and she wasn't having any of it. My grandmother, however, didn't believe in abortion. I stood in the kitchen between the two of them with tears in my eyes, my grandmother looking at me with a stern face and my mother lecturing me. I wanted my baby with everything in me, but my mother wouldn't back down for one minute.

I was about five months pregnant and thought for sure it would be too late to abort the baby. My mother took me to Kings County Hospital. At our counseling session with the nurse, I sat there scared with tears in my eyes, hoping that this lady would say, "It's too late—she's too far gone to have the procedure!" Being so young and not really understanding what I was about to get myself into, all I kept thinking was that I was getting ready to lose my baby.

After the counseling session, the nurse brought me into a room and asked me to take off my clothes and put on a hospital gown. The nurse then explained that this would be a two-day procedure. It was the worst two days of my life. The pain was unbearable. The moment they injected me with fluids, my baby began to slowly die. On the second day, still fighting through the pain, I ran out of the room and down a long hallway, crying and screaming. I ran into a bathroom and into one of the stalls, throwing my body on the bathroom floor, punching the floor of this dirty bathroom as I continued to cry.

Minutes later, I noticed two sets of feet standing next to me. I looked up, and it was my mother and a good friend of hers standing over me. They picked me up from the floor and walked me back to my room. The pain was increasing, and I was terrified.

As we went back into the room, the nurse was shouting, "It's time to push!" I was even more petrified.

The nurse laid me on a stretcher and told me to begin to push. All I wanted was for the pain to stop! So I began to push as hard as I could. Then all of a sudden, another nurse said to me in my ear, "Don't look down at the baby once you push it out!" She added, "It will torment you!"

I said to myself, *Lady, please, I want to see my baby!*

On that last push, my deceased baby came out. I looked down at my lifeless baby, who I'd wanted so badly, and there was a direct eye contact. I can still see this very small baby the size of the palm of my hand with its hands up in the air, her little fingers stretched apart.

That nurse was right. That one look at my baby tormented me for years. I would be in my house hearing a baby crying from the other room, and I would run to see where the crying was coming from. This went on for years until I finally let my daughter go.

The lifestyle my grandmother wanted for me was totally opposite from the way I was living. It got to the point where

I was completely out of control and getting kicked out of most of the schools I went to, However, I came from such a completely good family, no one would ever think that I would conduct myself the way I did. I was taught well.

I can remember many nights coming home high in the middle of the night and knocking on my grandmother's door, only for her to open the door and look me in the eye, knowing that I was high. I remember some nights walking past her bedroom high out of my mind, hoping that she was sleeping so she wouldn't see me like this. As I would slowly walk past her bedroom, I would see her sitting on the edge of her bed rocking back and forth with her hands folded together, praying within herself.

Grandma never said much to me about my bad behavior. All I can remember seeing her do was sit on the edge of her bed rocking back and forth.

A year after my abortion, I got pregnant again and gave birth to a son. I decided to slow down doing what I wanted to do and do what was right for him, so I got a job working at Lady Foot Locker in Midtown Manhattan. My family was so proud of me for making the decision to get a job. I really wanted to change my life, but I was unsatisfied with the wages I was getting from this job. I was so used to making fast money and having what I wanted that I became frustrated and decided to set up the store to get robbed.

I waited for a day where I was on schedule to work the early morning shift and would be in the store alone. I had one of my male friends come in and rob the store just to sell the sneakers to make extra money. My manager and the other workers never knew what happened; they just thought that someone had come into the store on my shift and robbed it. I still had my job, but later I quit and went back to doing what I wanted to do: make fast money. Although I wanted better for my son, I was so used to making fast money.

My son's first birthday came around, and I had just turned nineteen years old. I was still living in my grandma's house.

Chapter 3

One of my childhood best friends insisted that I talk to this guy she knew. My son's father had gotten locked up for eight years when I was four months pregnant. I was too much into the street and making my money and focusing on my son to get involved in any relationship. Still, my girlfriend insisted on getting me and this guy she knew together. She kept pushing until it happened.

One day, while we were sitting in front of my grandmother's building, she noticed the guy she was trying to hook me up with talking to some other guys across the park. She told me to look as she pointed her finger toward him. I told her again I wasn't interested, but she insisted on calling him over anyway.

He walked over, and she introduced us. He was fresh out of jail, fine, tall, dark, and handsome. The moment she introduced us and we locked eyes, it was love at first sight. From that day, we never left each other's side. We were together every day, getting acquainted with one another and enjoying each other's company. He was very handsome, charming, sweet, and loved my son. That was a plus to me.

Months passed by, and before my eyes, the guy I had spent so much time with got into trouble and got locked up. I thought to myself, *Oh boy, here we go again, back to square one now.* I found myself going on visits and accepting his phone calls. I was in love, but I wasn't nobody's fool.

I remember one time when I went to visit him, he came out of nowhere and asked me to have his baby! Remember, it had only been a couple of months since I met him. I looked at him and smiled and said, "Are you kidding me! I still live at home with my grandmother and with a one-year-old child. Where am I going to put another baby?" Nah! Grandma didn't raise no fool.

I told him that neither one of us was in a situation to have a baby, but this guy didn't stop with this baby stuff due to the fact that he didn't have any children of his own and wanted to have a child. He promised me that he would take care of me and find us a place to stay when he got out of jail. Coming from someone in his situation—no job, in jail, and talking about a baby!—I just laughed. What he said to me went in one ear and out the other.

One day at my grandmother's house, there was trouble, and I just couldn't take it anymore. I wanted to leave right then and there. As I was packing my things, someone knocked on the door. Grandma opened it, and as I looked down the hall to see who it was, to my surprise, it was my boyfriend! He was home. He looked at me, saw that I was upset, and said, "Let's go!" I didn't ask questions. I just left.

We took a train ride to Midtown Manhattan. After we got off the train, we walked a few blocks to a residential area. I was thinking to myself, *Where are we going?* But I still didn't ask any questions. I just followed.

We walked into a building where there was a doorman. *Okay*, I said to myself, *where are we and whose house are we going to?* We got on the elevator to the seventh floor. Then we walked up to a door and stopped. He didn't ring the bell, so I looked at him like, *Okay?* And he looked at me and then put his hand in his pocket and pulled out a set of keys.

I said to him, "Whose apartment is this?"

He said, "It's yours. Open the door!"

I was thinking to myself, *How in the world did he pull this off on the same day he was released from jail?* I thought it was a joke, but I took the key and unlocked the door. My eyes opened wide as I looked around the apartment. Wow! A huge three-bedroom two-bath unfurnished apartment on 26th Street and First Avenue. What a big change from where I came from!

I was so excited. I was nineteen years old with my first apartment, and I was happy!

However, my mother and grandmother were not happy about this at all. In the back of my mind, I just wanted to get out of the projects. I left my grandmother's house with my son. I just wanted something totally different, so I went on and started my own life.

I can remember the first night we shared the apartment together, we had no furniture. Neither one of us had a job, but I still had my hustle. We were young and in love.

Months passed, and I became pregnant with my second son. The drinking and the smoking and the hustling stopped, and I became a stay-at-home mother. We were a happy family. Everything was going so good, I just couldn't believe what had happened to me. It was like a dream come true.

Nine months later, I had my second son. My boyfriend was extremely happy to become a father. He had a hustle on the side to make money for his family. It wasn't that much, but we made it work. We always had plenty of food in the refrigerator and kept a roof over our heads.

He was the type of guy who was always on the streets. He met some guy there who hustled with him—they sold T-shirts together. He didn't take the time to get to know this guy; he trusted this guy's friendship. He would bring this guy over to the apartment every once in a while. I would get upset about it because I didn't like strangers in and out of the house. We had children, and we didn't know this guy.

Long story short, the guy became very jealous of my boyfriend and tried to rob him of his chain. He beat the guy up, and after the fight, the guy told him, "I will be back!"

Well, the guy kept his promise and came back.

On that day, I was in the apartment with one of my girlfriends. We were cooking and listening to music; the music was up very loud. My younger son was just a baby sitting in his walker directly in front of the front door of the apartment.

I heard a voice whisper in my ear saying, *Take the baby from in front of the door!* I stopped and looked around, not knowing where the voice was coming from and why it was telling me to move my baby from in front of the door. But again, I heard a voice tell me to move the baby from the

13

front door. This time the voice was louder than the loud music we were playing in the house

So I immediately walked over to the front door, took my baby out of the walker, and walked over to the living room couch and sat down, The moment I sat down, we heard a loud sound coming from out in the hallway; it sounded like gunshots! My girlfriend and I looked at each other and slowly walked over to the front door, just to see what all the noise was about. That's when we noticed the bullet holes covering the front door and the hallway wall.

We immediately started panicking. At that time, our phone was off, and neither one of us had a cell phone to call 911. So we cut the music off and waited quietly. We listened to hear if the person who shot up the door was still in the hallway. As we listened, we heard the elevator door open and the sound of police officers' walkie-talkies. We slowly opened the door and looked out in the hallway.

There were so many cops walking toward my apartment door with their guns drawn! They told us to put our hands up and not to move. We did what they said, and then we finally got the chance to explain to the officers that someone had just shot up the door. A police report was made, and thank God the doorman of the building was able to give the officers a video of the guy getting on the elevator and getting off on our floor. Just a few days later, the guy turned himself in to the cops.

Thank God that at that moment we had the music blasting, because according to a witness, the guy was ringing my doorbell like a madman hoping that someone would open the door. Normally when someone rang the bell, I would just open the door without knowing who it was. That night would've been different—he probably would have blown my head off. We stayed in our apartment, and the building manager gave us a bulletproof door. Nothing like that had ever happened before.

A few years went by, and everything was still going well. I would go to my grandmother's house from time to time to visit but not too often. My boyfriend really didn't want me around the projects at all, so I stayed home. We never really did too much outside activity after I had my second son. We would just stay home and have movie nights most of the time, and I would cook, clean, and take care of my family.

It was all good in the beginning, but anybody would get tired of just cooking, cleaning, and taking care of kids all day without any space or time of their own. I wanted to go out. I wanted to visit my family more often. I wanted to hang out with my friends every once in a while, just to get a break from the family. But that was something he didn't want me to do. He never wanted me to leave his side, and of course, he didn't want to do anything but stay in the apartment.

As time went on, I began to feel isolated. We were both new to the area where we'd moved, but he was getting more acquainted with the guys in the neighborhood. He was also introduced to a business opportunity with a well-known record company and became a road manager for a rap artist. I thought to myself, *Okay, this is great. We are really going to be set!* We talked about moving from where we were living and getting a better place.

Through this artist, he met a lot of famous people. Famous people were calling the apartment. Famous people came to our home. He had a VIP pass for every private party. The money was growing. He was going on tours, and I was excited!

However, I was still at home. He took me to a few VIP parties and introduced me to some famous people, but for the most part, I played the part of a stay-at-home mom.

Chapter 4

My grandmother told me the day I left home that if it didn't work out with me and my boyfriend, I could always come home. There were times when I just wanted to throw in the towel. I felt alone. His true colors began to come out, and we began to argue back and forth around the kids.

I would call home to my grandmother often just to talk to her on the phone and let her know everything that was going on and how I was feeling. She would always tell me, "Baby, take it to the Lord!" So we would pray over the phone and things would calm down for a little while. Then it would pick back up again—the arguing, the disagreement, the cheating. It just wouldn't stop!

He became big-headed, and it was all about him. However, I loved him and wanted to keep my family together. He had so many people who wanted to be around him because of who he was and the job that he had. He was so much into the work that he was doing until that was all he could really focus on.

I trusted him, because at that time, that was all we had: one another. We'd agreed when we first met that he would be the breadwinner. He promised me everything from soup to nuts, and I believed him. I agreed that he would work and go on tour because of all the things he'd promised me and my son.

Unfortunately, among the things the money and the VIP parties brought was *women*. I thought that he would never cheat on me. We were together every day before he got the job. We built our home together from nothing. I trusted him, and when the truth came out, it hurt!

I wound up getting pregnant for the third time with a set of twin boys. I had already put it in my mind that I was done having children once I'd had my second son, but God had other plans. My sons were everything to me, and I wanted the best for them. I thought I was making all the right decisions, but apparently I wasn't.

At this point, my boyfriend was doing whatever he wanted to do. The disrespect grew worse, and he broke my heart. There was another woman pregnant, and she kept the baby. I never in a million years thought that he would hurt me in that way.

Our relationship was over. I decided to move out of state with my sons. I had no job and no money. I felt embarrassed, used, and betrayed. By being a stay-at-home mom and allowing him to be the breadwinner, I had set myself up for failure. I became very angry at myself for allowing myself to boomerang into a situation like this, but love made me do a lot of things that I normally wouldn't.

I was broken inside, but my heart wanted my family together. I was young with four little boys. I thought that if I walked away from him, I would struggle real bad, and I didn't want that for my sons. But I had no other choice. The pain that came from being around him and living in that house was awful. I got tired of the cheating, the verbal abuse, and the lies. I just wanted out!

So I came up with a plan. As he continued to cheat on me with so many different women, going to parties, turning his phone off, staying out all night, and leaving me alone with our children, I was home thinking of a way to get out of this relationship that hurt me so bad. I began to make phone calls to different places out of state, looking for a place of my own for me and my sons. I was successful in finding a place in the Poconos, and I went for it.

One evening, I packed up everything I owned in a U-Haul truck I'd rented. But when I brought my sons downstairs to get in the truck and drive to our new apartment, my U-Haul truck was gone. Someone had stolen it, along with everything we owned. Now I really had nothing.

I thought to myself, *Now that I have lost everything, maybe I should stay in my apartment.* But things were too crazy with me and my boyfriend. I mean, I would cry day and night. I would wake up crying and go to sleep crying. To say that I was depressed was an understatement. There was no way I could stay there with the woman he had gotten pregnant living one floor down from us. If I stayed, I would wind up in jail for trying to kill this girl, and it just wasn't worth it. I refused to leave my sons alone while serving time in jail.

So I moved out of state with my children, found an apartment, got a job, registered the boys in school, and got a car. In less than a year, I was doing well for myself. Of course I thought about him, but I had gotten used to living without him. But he came from time to time to visit our sons, and he talked me into forgiving him. He told me he was no longer involved with the girl he had gotten pregnant. So I took him back. I wanted my family together more than anything, and I figured we were in a new state, so things could be better. We had a new start.

Chapter 5

To seal our new start, he asked me to marry him. I had waited years for this moment, so of course I said yes. New state, new home, and I'm married! I was happy again.

It felt right for a while, but he just couldn't remain faithful. After he had gotten the woman in New York pregnant, a lot of my feelings for him had left. I just wanted my family together, but marrying him was the worst mistake of my life.

The arguing continued, forgiveness after forgiveness, and my depression set back in. I had lost my apartment due to financial issues, so we moved into another place in the same state—only to lose that place too because it was too much for me and he wasn't working anymore. So we left and moved to another place in the same state.

He cheated on me again—and not only cheated, he was

sleeping with a woman I had met in the area we were living in. I felt sorry for her because her husband was very abusive, so I allowed this woman and her children into my home to stay for a while so she didn't have to deal with her husband. And while I was working trying to keep up with the bills, my husband and this woman enjoyed my bed together.

So now I was ready to kill someone. That was the last straw with him. I just couldn't do it anymore. Come to find out she wasn't the only one he was sleeping with; he was sleeping with her close friend as well. This friend was a young girl I would often drive to work. I mean, being with someone and they cheat on you hurts. But being married to someone who cheats is a different feeling.

I told him I was done with him and that was the last straw. I'd had enough. The more he cheated on me, the fewer feelings I had for him. Over the years that I stayed with him, there were so many people who talked to me from their hearts and told me to walk away from him, that he was no good for me, and that God had something better for me. For so long, I just couldn't let go. Love caused me to stay. But finally, I left my husband. I was back on my own again.

I struggled out-of-state with my boys. I had no support from my husband at all. It got so bad that we were living in our house without lights and water. The twins were still in Pampers at the time. One of the twins needed his Pamper changed. I had to clean him, and I had run out of baby wipes, so I got a rag and looked for something to wet it with. I barely had anything in my refrigerator, but I noticed half a bottle of Pepsi. I had no other choice but to wet the rag with the soda just to clean my baby. I was hurt. All I did was cry. I felt helpless.

But no matter what, I kept on standing. I didn't allow myself to give up. I kept telling myself that things would get better for us.

Finally, though, the weight got too heavy for me to bear. The bills became too much for me to handle, and we got evicted. I was broken inside. All I wanted to do, like any other parent, was to have a steady residence and a decent income to support my children. I mean, I felt horrible. I felt like life had cheated me. I was a good person. I gave, I helped, I supported. I was there for people. I didn't want it all, just a roof over my children's head. I wanted to be able to feed them when they were hungry and enjoy my life.

Things went from bad to worse. After we got evicted from the house, we had nowhere to go. The money I was making from my job was not enough for us to move into a new place right away. The only thing we had was my van. Most of our clothes and furniture went into storage, which we lost shortly after that due to nonpayment. I had no other choice. I drove around with my children in the van day after day and night after night.

A friend I'd met in the neighborhood had a big house that her mother left her. She lived there with her husband, her daughter, and her son. It was a two-family house, so I thought that with her having plenty of room, we could possibly stay a night or two at her house until I came up with somewhere else to stay. I drove my van into her driveway and knocked on the door.

She answered, and as I stood in her doorway, I explained my situation—that we had just gotten evicted and had nowhere to go. I asked if it would be okay for her to take us in for a day or two. She said that she was unable to take us in, but we were more than welcome to sleep in my van in her driveway.

My heart dropped as I stared at her with a blank face. I thanked her and walked away with tears in my eyes. I got back in my van and drove off. As I was backing out of her driveway, tears flooded down my face. I was so hurt! How could a mother with children be so cold to another mother in this type of situation?

I remembered all the times my grandmother would tell me to take every situation to the Lord. So, as I continued to drive away, I began to pray within myself. I prayed, but there was one thing that stood out to me, and that was, *Lord, where do you want us to park to sleep?* The Lord answered my prayer that night. He led us to a major bus stop parking lot, and we parked there. I parked the van in a corner where no one could see us.

It was pitch dark and bleeding cold. I took the clothes we had in the back of the van and put them all over my children just to keep them warm. I sat in the driver's seat and asked the Lord to protect me and my children as we slept through the night. I opened my Bible, read a verse, and fell asleep.

I woke up, and it was the next morning! My sons had to go to school, and I had to go to work. There was nowhere for us to wash and to prepare ourselves for work and school, so I decided to drive to a nearby gas station. We took a quick birdbath, washed our faces, and brushed our teeth. I dropped my sons off at school and went to work.

Every morning, we would drive to a nearby gas station to take a birdbath. There was a day when I took the kids to school, and I was off from work. I was so exhausted; I hadn't gotten any sleep because I was too afraid to fall asleep in the van with my boys out in the street and going through too much trauma to get a good night's rest. I prayed and asked the Lord where to park my van just so that I could take a nap. He led me to a nearby public park. I parked the van, read my Bible for a little while, laid the seat back in the van, and took a nap until it was time to pick my sons up from school.

We lived like this for at least two weeks, until I got tired of it. I decided it was time to head back to New York. I felt ashamed and embarrassed; I didn't want to show my face to all my family, especially my grandmother. I didn't want to disappoint her. But I didn't have a choice. I just couldn't deal with being homeless and sleeping in my van in the bitter cold with my children anymore. I never thought I would have to go through all of this.

At this point, my grandmother was very sick. When I walked into her house with my children, she was sitting at the kitchen table in her wheelchair. I sat on the opposite side of the table from her for a while. Grandma didn't say a word to me as she sat and ate her dinner, but she kept looking up at me.

Finally, she said, "Why are you here?"

I was at a loss for words. I didn't answer her. I didn't want to worry or disappoint her. She was going through enough. I just looked at her with tears in my eyes and a smirk on my face. At that time, Grandma was so sick that her words were limited, but she knew something was wrong because I had come home.

One day at Grandma's house, after bathing her and changing her clothes, I was about to walk away from her bedside when she looked at me and said, "How many bedrooms do you need?"

My response was, "Huh?"

And she said again, "How many bedrooms do you need?"

I looked down at her as she lay on her deathbed and said, "I need three bedrooms, Grandma."

Grandma put her hand out to me, and I put my hand in hers. She closed her eyes and said a prayer for me within herself. After she prayed, she looked up at me and said, "Don't you ever forget about God!"

And I said to her, as I held her hand and looked into her eyes, "Grandma, I promise I won't." I found strength in my grandmother's prayer and what she said to me. I stayed there for a few days to help take care of my grandmother, and then we left.

I gave my sister a phone call and explained to her what the boys and I were going through. She immediately told me to come stay at her house until I got back on my feet. I was so happy to be in a nice warm home and to be able to take a hot shower, feed my children a good meal, and finally get some rest. After two weeks, my husband got in contact with me again. Between him and his slick talk and me still having feelings for him, he wound up coming to stay with us at my sister's house.

My sister only had a one-bedroom apartment that she shared with her son along with me, my husband, and our four boys. Things there didn't last long. We were only there for a couple of months; the space was just too small. My sister talked me into going to a homeless shelter. For the life of me, I didn't want to do that. I knew nothing at all

26

about living in a shelter. All kinds of thoughts ran through my mind. I said, "God, will things ever get better for me and my family?"

We had to go. We had taken advantage of my sister's space long enough. The homeless shelter wasn't too bad, but we were around a lot of people who were involved with a lot of crazy things. We also had a curfew to be back in the shelter. We made the best of it. At least my boys and I were off the street.

My husband was also there with us. I remember one nice summer night when my husband and our boys were invited to a barbecue. Being responsible and knowing that we had a curfew at the shelter, I said that we needed to leave the barbecue. But my husband refused. He wanted to stay and enjoy his friends. I got very upset and told him that if he did not leave with us or we were not on time to make our curfew, he would be discharged from the shelter. He told me that he was staying at the barbecue.

As I walked away with my children, I felt so bad that tears came to my eyes. Here I was, alone again. This man never ceased to amaze me. I had to travel alone with my children on the train to get from Brooklyn to the Bronx to make our curfew, because we had nowhere to stay if we were kicked out, and I refused to let that to happen again. How could a man not take care of his responsibility, especially in a situation like this, when it involved his children having a roof over their head? I made it back to the shelter in time, but my husband was discharged.

Shortly after that, while I was at the shelter, I received a phone call from my mother that my grandmother had passed away. It felt like a part of me was taken away. I was devastated! My grandmother was the one who raised me, the one who prayed for me, the one I confided in, the one who comforted me when I needed it. I felt all kinds of emotions. I even became angry that she had left me. She was the one who kept me going! She would encourage me all the time and always wanted the best for me.

I was left in charge of doing my grandmother's home-going service. After all she had done for me, I was so excited, even though I was devastated that she had left me. Grandma was laid to rest, and the home-going service was awesome.

After spending about a year in the shelter, we got the keys to our apartment. Man, I was so happy. Finally, I was back on my feet. But my husband wasn't letting go of the marriage, and he managed to find out where we were living. He came to visit us, and of course, I was not happy about that. I was done with the relationship. It was no longer about me wanting to keep my family together. I just wanted to be alone. I had found peace. It was just too much with him being around.

Of course, he wanted to move in, but that was unacceptable to me. My feelings for him were gone. He ended up staying a few nights against my will. I didn't want to fight with him and cause a scene in the new place. The neighborhood we were in was very quiet, and I didn't want any problems.

I continued to ask him to leave, and he refused. He was very controlling and still abusive. I was very intimidated by his actions. His behavior went from bad to worse. He definitely had me in a place where I was scared to confront him and to stand up for myself. Deep down on the inside of me, I didn't want anything to do with him. I was disgusted by the things he had already put us through over the years. He knew I was done with him, and that just made his anger grow.

My leaving him was something he just couldn't accept. My new place that I had sacrificed so much to get became a place of depression. I was miserable in my own home. The arguing started again. The cops were called, but of course, he told them we were married and that he was a resident there. The cops told me there was nothing they could do. I was so upset that it was his word against mine. At this point, I really wanted out of this relationship.

Marrying him was the worst thing I could have done. I felt trapped, unappreciated, and unloved. I should have walked away from this relationship years before, but love kept me there.

I hadn't been in this new place a year, and all hell had broken loose the moment he showed up at my doorstep. The cops continued to be called. I was so embarrassed. One time I called the cops because of physical abuse, and before they could get there, he ran off. This was a Saturday evening, and he didn't come back that night. The next morning, I decided that my sons and I would go to church. We enjoyed the service and headed home.

One of my twin boys was in his room changing in his clothes, and he yelled at me from his room, "Mommy, Daddy's in the closet!"

My heart dropped. I had no idea what he was going to do to get back at me for calling the cops on him the night before. I walked into the room, and he was sitting in my son's closet. He was hiding there I don't know how long, but he was waiting for us to come home.

Things began to get very scary. He definitely wasn't the guy I met in the beginning. I mean, things were getting really bad with him. I was living in fear of the man who was supposed to protect and love me.

The physical and mental abuse really wore me out. It got to the point where he started making threats to kill me. He actually told my children, "I am going to kill your mother." He would threaten me in that way all the time. He would say, "Now you're going to church, and you think that you're going to become somebody successful in life, but before that happens, I will kill you! And you're going to leave here in a body bag!"

I began to think I'd been sleeping with the enemy all these years. Some nights he would turn off all the lights in the house, unplug the phones, and have me in one of the bedrooms in the house and torment me. One night, he chased me out of the house at about three in the morning, waving a hammer. I was running down the block and around cars with my nightgown on to get away from him. I called the cops, and like before, he took off running. He was afraid to go to jail.

I just couldn't live like that anymore. One night, I took my children, and we drove to the precinct. Out of fear, I made another police report and explained to the cops that I was afraid of him and he was constantly threatening to kill me. The cops made another police report and followed me home.

When we got there, my house was demolished. He had basically destroyed everything. My furniture was upside down. A window was broken out. Things were just a mess. I began to clean up the mess he had made. After the police had left the house, my phone began to ring. It was my aunt. She told me to get out of the house. My husband had just called her and told her and my mother that he was on his way to kill me.

I had never felt such fear. I grabbed my children, got in my car, and drove straight out of state, just to get away from him. I was scared to death! He had sabotaged everything I'd worked so hard to get. I stayed at one of my girlfriends' houses for a couple of weeks. After that, I went back to New York and entered a domestic violence shelter for my protection. I had lost it all again. I was devastated, and so were my children.

After that, I didn't see my husband for a while. I managed to get another job, and my children were in a new school. I never gave up on my children or myself. I continued to strive and work hard to get myself and my children where we needed to be in our lives. Although we were in a domestic violence shelter, I found peace at night knowing he would not be able to locate us.

However, going to work some days, I would be afraid, hoping not to bump into him. I would walk down the street some days, and if someone was walking behind me, I would instantly jump and turn around out of fear. I mean, he had messed me up really bad.

One day, a coworker and I went out for lunch. We were in a Chinese restaurant ordering our food, and I turned around to see my husband staring through the glass door looking at me. I was scared for my life. I had explained to my coworker just bits and pieces of what I'd had to go through with my husband, so she already had an insight into what type of guy he was.

31

I said to her, "Oh my God! That's my husband!"

She confronted him as we walked back to the job and told him that if he did not leave the premises, she was going to call the cops. She told him, "You're not gonna do anything to her as long as I'm around."

He walked away and left. I made another police report, and I made it back to the shelter safely. I was transferred to a different site on the job due to the fact that he found me and knew where I worked. I was clueless as to how he had found me.

Shortly after, I found out that he was staying at my mother's house, so I had to stay away from there. I was limited in where I could go: just the domestic violence shelter, work, my sons' school, and looking for another place to stay. I kept myself limited in the things I did and the places I would go. I never wanted to run into him again.

One day while I was in the shelter, I needed to go to the store. I took the elevator downstairs, where I was approached by one of the security guards. The guard stopped me and took me into an office in the building. There, he explained that a young man had just come into the shelter asking about me before running past the security guard and up the exit stairs. As I was going down on the elevator, he was running up the stairs. The cops were called, but somehow he managed to get out of the building before they showed up.

There was no way I was going to live the rest of my life like this. I became very angry. I learned that he had been following me for months. He was driving around watching me. He knew where the shelter was. He knew where I worked. He knew where my children went to school. I'd had no idea I was being watched by him all that time.

I got to my breaking point. I'd had all I was going to take from him. So I made a call to him as I stood on the corner by the shelter. I was crying and yelling. I was angry and tired of him following me and threatening me and making my life and my sons' lives miserable. I asked him where he was, because now I was looking for him to kill him. My mind snapped. I refused to live that way anymore and allow him to take me away from my children.

While I was asking him where he was at, his voice softened up. Now *he* was scared. He'd never heard me like that before. He knew that I meant what I said. His life was about to be over. I told him that I was going to kill him.

After that phone call, he backed off of me. Shortly after that, I got another apartment—a three-bedroom, just as my grandmother had prayed for. After we'd moved into our new place, I decided that I had to get counseling for myself and my sons. We were damaged from all that we'd had to go through.

The counseling really helped us out a lot. But it took me years to get over all the hell that I'd had to endure over the course of the years—even from my childhood! I had kept things buried in my heart and swept all the mess under the rug. I suffered for years by allowing the hurt and pain to take over.

I remembered all the times my grandmother had tried her hardest to get me to stay in church—all of the countless hours of praying she did for me, the talks she had with me, and most importantly, what she said to me on her deathbed: "Don't you ever forget about God!"

So I decided to give myself back to the Lord. I had no one else to turn to. No one understood me like my grandmother. She was so determined that before she left this earth, I would have a relationship with the Lord, and my soul would be saved. Grandma paved a great way for me. As much as I fought against her about going to church, I am ever so grateful today for what she did.

Her constant faith in God and her prayers made me the woman I am today. I can remember as a child seeing her praying and her prayers coming to pass. She demonstrated that the Lord was real. She taught me from a distance and made sure I was ready for the battles that would come in my life.

After Grandma's transition, I learned to stand and pray for myself. Grandma departed, and God grew closer. I had to learn how to walk with the Lord for myself. As the Lord has grown closer to me, I have experienced such a walk with him. He took me further than my grandmother could ever take me.

This walk with the Lord was deeper than I thought it would be. He showed me things that blew my mind, and he brought me out of things I could never have seen my way out of on my own. I struggled so much with building a relationship with the Lord because of all of the mistreatment, the letdowns, the betrayal, and the violations I went through for so many years and from so many people who were supposed to protect and love me.

God is the best thing that ever happened to me. He has never let me down. He was there with me all the time. Even from my childhood, he was there. It was his divine plan and purpose for my life. I grew in the Lord and became a faithful member of the church. The Lord began to sharpen my gifts and show me a lot of things in the spirit.

Chapter 6

One day, I went out to do some grocery shopping. As I was leaving the supermarket, I saw a few guys standing outside who drove taxicabs. With all the groceries I had bought, I needed a cab to get back home.

One guy came over to me and said, "Hi, do you need a cab? I can give you a ride."

I saw that he was holding a Bible in his hand and thought, *Wow, okay, this is a blessing!*

As he was driving me home, we began to talk about the Lord and what church we both belonged to. I thought to myself, *Okay, he's a Christian, and I'm very well familiar with the church he attends* (a very powerful ministry). I asked him if he had a business card. I figured that I would call him whenever I needed a cab.

When we pulled up into the driveway of my house, he

got out of the car and was kind enough to help me bring my bags to the doorway of my house. Then he stood in the doorway and said, chuckling, "Wow, I definitely feel the prayers in here."

We continued to talk for a few minutes, and then I paid him for the ride home and he left. I was used to taking cabs, because where I live, that's the easiest and fastest way to get around. The very next day, I needed a cab, so I grabbed his business card and gave him a call. He came right away.

He became my personal cab driver. We would laugh and talk about a lot of different things. There were often times when I ran out to take care of some business or was running late to pick up my boys from school, so I would call him to run certain errands for me. It was never a problem for him. Every time I called, he was available.

We had built a good relationship and become good friends, but then it went from dating to him asking me to marry him! I wasn't ready for that. I really enjoyed his company though. All we did was laugh at different things and talk about the Lord. Sometimes we would have Bible study at my house, and my boys even enjoyed his company. That was very unusual for them, being that the only man they were used to was their father.

As time went on, things about this guy began to change. He started to act very strange and say weird things that just didn't make sense. Then the Lord exposed him!

It started one day when he came to my house for lunch. I was cooking as he sat at the counter by the dining room reading his Bible. He decided he wanted to have Bible study with me. So I agreed—after I finished cooking.

He gave me the choice to pick out what we were going

to study. I decided that we should study the book of Genesis, so I had my Bible open to that book. As I was reading, I happened to look up at him, and he was just sitting there smiling. I noticed that his Bible was open but not to the book of Genesis, so I asked him to turn his Bible to that book.

He said to me with a smile on his face, "I don't have it!"

I said, "Why not?"

I grabbed his Bible to turn it to the book of Genesis, and lo and behold, the whole book of Genesis was gone. I asked him what happened. "Where is the book of Genesis?"

He smiled and said, "It is under my bed!"

I was confused by that but didn't really think too much of it. As time went by, though, the Lord began to show me more and more about this guy.

There was another day when he was at my house and reading his Bible like always. Every time he was around me, that's all we would do, other than him taking me on errands. On this particular day, he started talking about his son, and he began to tell me—while laughing!—that his son was a drug dealer.

I said, "Why are you laughing? You should be praying for him!"

At that moment, I walked into my bathroom. When I walked out of the bathroom and returned to the living room, I saw him lying flat on his back wiggling around like a snake.

I called out his name and yelled, "Get up! What are you doing?" I thought, *Okay, this guy is acting really weird.* So now I had concerns.

Another day while he was at my house, he came out

of nowhere and said to me, "I can't get you like I can get to other women. You're too strong!" He continued to say that he had women ministers who did street ministry with him, giving out tracts and praying for people in different train stations. As he was talking to me about these different women doing street ministry with him, he became very angry, saying, "You Christians don't listen!"

I was like, "Excuse me? What did you say?" Now I was offended! At this point, I said to myself, *Hold up! Something is off with this guy.* I had to go into prayer and ask the Lord to show me who this guy really was.

The moment I got into prayer, a light flashed, and a python appeared in front of my face. This python was very angry at me. It came very close to my face in a big image as I stood there looking eye to eye at him. I noticed that a lot of venom was pouring out of his mouth. I said, "God, what in the world?" All of this time, this guy was walking around proclaiming he was a man of God, doing street ministry and praying for people.

Now I was upset about the fact that he was around my sons. The Lord began to speak to me about this person and told me not to allow him to lay one finger on me. The Lord continued to speak and gave me a message to give to this man. I agreed to deliver the Lord's message. The Lord told me to ask him if he was ready to die.

When he came back to the house, he just sat in his car in the driveway. He called me from his cell phone and ask me to come out. So I told him I would be right out—to give me a minute. When I walked out to his car and sat on the passenger side, he was laid back in the driver's seat with his arms behind his head and his eyes closed.

I said to him, "The Lord wants me to tell you something."

Once I said that, he sat up quickly, and his eyes grew wide. He asked, "What is it?"

I said, "The Lord asked me to tell you not to lay one finger on me."

His eyes got even bigger, and he replied, "Wow! The Lord told me the same thing not too long ago."

He went back to lay back in his seat, and I said, "Wait, there's more."

He said, "What is it?"

I replied, "The Lord said, 'Are you ready to die?'"

He jumped up quickly with his arm stretched out in front of him and his fingers far apart. His face was full of fear. He began to yell, "No, no, no, no! I'm not ready to die!"

I got out of the car and walked back into my house. I was so confused. What just happened out there? From that point on, he was never allowed back into my house at all. I continued to pray, and God continued to expose him.

Another day when I was out grocery shopping, he came across my mind. At this point, I was still upset with him. So I decided to give him a call just to express how I felt. As soon as he picked up the phone, I began to express myself, and he just laughed at me. I gave him some choice words and hung up on him.

That night, I fell asleep and had a dream. The Lord showed me that this particular guy was trying to put a hex on me and my boys. I saw him with a red scarf tied around his head. He had some type of stripes on each side of his face, and there was something that looked like DJ equipment. On it was what looked like two big round silver plates that were spinning very fast. He was standing in front of this with his hands close together. What I saw in his hands was some kind of white or beige powder.

I saw him take the powder that was in his hand and blow it to where these two round silver things were spinning. The powder was blowing toward me and my sons. At that time, in the dream, I became very weak, to the point where I couldn't get up to pray.

I woke up from the dream and ran immediately into my son's room. When I got to his bedside, his body was bent. His arms were bent backward behind his head and his legs were also bent. I laid hands on him quickly and began to break the power off of him. Whatever this guy tried to do, it was broken. After that, I was fighting mad!

The Lord showed me in the dream that this guy was a warlock. His cover-up was attending church services and carrying the Bible and praying for people in train stations. He was a wolf in sheep's clothing. That was the first time I had ever experienced the enemy in that way.

Chapter 7

Despite all the pain and hurt I'd been through in my life, I remained faithful to God. I attended church faithfully, praying and trusting God with my whole heart. Still trying to recover from all that I'd been through, I was broken and scared, with deep wounds only God could heal.

My grandmother taught me that church was a safe haven for me—a place I could go for healing, comfort, and love. I felt safe there, and as I began to move forward in God, things were going great. Most of my trials and tribulations ceased a little. However, there will always be the nasty folks, the haters, and the gossipers wherever you go.

I said to myself, *People are going to be people!* I continued to pray and trust God through it all. And after years had passed, things took a major turn. The Lord began to show me things that blew my mind. I just couldn't believe what he was showing me. I was in great unbelief! The dreams and visions were too much for me to handle.

However, I continued to be faithful in this ministry. The more the Lord showed me, the more I found myself praying. It got so intense that the enemy began to act up, using the leader in the ministry to verbally abuse me. So many times I walked out of the sanctuary in the middle of a sermon just to go to the bathroom and cry. I would feel so bad and embarrassed, to the point where I just wanted to leave the church.

But every time I wanted to give up, the Lord stopped me. I had to stay and take it. I couldn't understand why the Lord would allow me to stay in a place where I was being abused, but I realized there was a purpose in all of this.

I had a dream in which I saw two ladies walking into the church I was attending wearing long robes. They both had Bibles in their hands. Being that I was one of the intercessors in the church, it was my responsibility to pray and watch over and make sure the church was in proper order. One day at home, I went into prayer about the situation, and the Lord showed me two different spirits that were not sent by God. I continued to pray and ask the Lord who they were, where they came from, and what was the purpose of them coming into this ministry.

He said, "The spirit of deception!"

As one of the intercessors of the church, it was my responsibility to open up in prayer for every service. Before the service started, I kept my eyes open watching the movement of these two individuals. They were very much secret agents in the church who were sent by the enemy. But

I knew who they were. The Lord had already exposed them to me before they got there.

Everyone was going on praising and worshiping God throughout the service. They didn't realize who was in our camp. These spirits came into the church speaking well of the Lord, giving their praise and their praise reports. The church was blindsided by their deceitful ways. Their hearts were far off from God. I was looking around like, *Lord, am I the only one who sees this?*

The mental abuse continued. In fact, it got worse. I sat in these services with tears in my eyes, just wanting to walk away from all of this madness. I found myself going home after services to cry and ask God, "Why? Why me, Lord?"

All he would say was, "I'm with you. Get back in there."

As time went on, it became worse, to the point where I just couldn't bear it anymore. However, my prayers only grew stronger, and the Lord was with me every step of the way. He defended and protected me. The more the Lord would show me who they were, the more they would attack me, but I kept coming.

I was humiliated and embarrassed all the time. They would try to discourage me. They wanted to control me. They became angrier with me when they couldn't. The Lord wouldn't allow it. It was all about control in this ministry, and we all know that control is not of God! So they tried to torment me service after service. But the Lord was always on my side. He would always defend me from their wicked ways.

If the leader didn't like me, the church didn't like me. It was crazy. It just wouldn't stop. I felt alone. I really didn't have anyone to talk to about this situation because basically, everyone praised this leader. I felt that no one would believe me anyway if I told them, so I kept it between me and God.

The hurt and the pain were horrible. Like, come on. If I can't trust the church, who can I trust? Besides, I had already been through enough, When I joined this church, I thought, *Yes, finally, I can get a break from all of the mess that I've dealt with out in the world*, but that wasn't the case. In fact, it hurt me even more, because it was the church.

I thought to myself, *Is this what my grandmother fought for all those years? To get me to go to church for this? No! Something is wrong!*

And it was! The devil ran this church. I finally understood why the Lord sent me there. It was for me to grow, to learn, and to become stronger and wiser in him. No matter what they tried to do to me, it would always fall through the cracks, because the Lord was with me. I began to excel in ministry, but it was never acknowledged. I was always overlooked and cast down.

One time after the church service was over, I was talking to one of the members of the church when one of the ladies who operated in the spirit of deception came up behind me and put me in a chokehold. I grabbed her arm for her to get off of me, and finally she let go. At this point, I was ready to fight. How dare she put her hands on me? She looked at me and walked away.

Now that these spirits were becoming physical with me, the torment just got worse. It got so bad that they began to operate their evil ways in the church. I just couldn't stand it. However, I learned so much by going through all of this.

The Lord allowed me to go through it all for ministry purposes. I mean, their hearts were far from God. They wanted me to bow down to their behavior, but I refused to participate in evildoing. I mean, it was bad, and I didn't want any part of it at all. The name-calling and laughing at me was crazy.

Chapter 8

The Lord called me to pray for a pastor who was in trouble. As I said yes to God, He began to lead me. I was under so much pressure with everything that was going on in this ministry. I needed to stay focused The Lord had me on a Pacific time to pray and fast for this pastor, and as I did so, things in my home became very intense.

I noticed that as the Lord took me deeper into prayer for this man of God, the attacks became even greater. The prayers were more intense, and the warfare was great. These spirits were very angry and came at me even stronger, to the point where they caused many problems around me to distract me and stop me from praying. But I would not stop.

This situation got really crazy. So much stuff was coming at me to stop me, but the Lord said, "Keep going!" As I prayed, the Lord showed me so much stuff that the enemy had put on this pastor. My goodness, the enemy wanted to take him out. The things that I saw were unbelievable.

One day, the Lord told me to get on my knees, put my face on my bedroom floor, and pray for this pastor. The moment I put my face to my floor and closed my eyes, I saw a big pit with flames of fire. It was hell. The devil had a special place for this man of God. The devil was ready for him, but the Lord had other plans.

I even saw, as I was praying, the man of God's car. As the Lord led me to pray there, I saw so many different spirits coming out of his car from the trunk, the hood of the car, under the wheels, the back and front seats. There were so many dark spirits leaping from out of his car. I believe they were trying to cause an accident to take him out. But God stopped it.

It got to the point where this leader no longer looked like himself, so I said to the Lord, "What is this? What is on this pastor?"

He said, "White and black magic." Witchcraft! It got to the point where they controlled his mind so he couldn't remember certain things.

This was something I had never experienced before. I can remember praying for hours at a time. Some days, I would pray hard warfare prayers for three hours. The Lord led me to pray in ways I never knew existed. Some days, I prayed all day long. I prayed different prayers, but each was a hard warfare prayer. The Lord was going after this pastor.

The prayers got so intense and so hard that my feet became swollen from walking the floor for hours. My knees would hurt so bad from kneeling down for hours at a time that I was no longer able to kneel in prayer. My body was extremely exhausted.

I was not allowed to go outside at all due to this assignment unless it was for church or, every once in a while, to go to the store. Then I had to be back in my place of prayer. This assignment was very strict, and the Lord was in full control.

The Lord had me praying for this individual every hour on the hour. The warfare toward me was great, but the Lord's hand was mighty in this battle. I was fighting chief demons that were on an assignment for this man of God. There were days when my body couldn't take it anymore. I was so worn out.

I have seen and heard so much in the spirit while in prayer. It was so crazy—those spirits did everything they could to try to stop me. But the Lord did not allow it to happen.

This went on for a little over a year. I can remember speaking in these unknown tongues. The sound of it was something I had never heard before, to the point where it scared me. I was at a place I didn't know of, but as long as the Lord was with me, I kept going.

I had so many visions as I continued praying, but there was one that amazed my eyes and encouraged me greatly throughout all of this. As I was on my knees praying, I saw the man of God I was praying for on his knees. His head was face down to the ground, and around his neck were chains connected to his wrists and his feet. There were demons standing all around him, tormenting him. Then I turned around and looked up, and out of the sky came Jesus sitting on a cloud with a sword in his right hand. He was moving toward the man of God.

Once the demons surrounding and tormenting this man of God saw Jesus coming toward them, they all took flight. The Lord never said a word. He showed up, and the demons were terrified. They took off running the moment they saw him coming.

In that moment, the chains that had this man of God bound instantly fell off of him. He immediately stood up on his feet. But when he stood up, he stood up in great power! He was free from the enemy.

There were so many encounters, so many visitations, and so much that I learned in all of this. Most importantly, I learned that when you are called to pray for someone's deliverance, you must be clean. You cannot help someone come out of something if you're struggling with the exact same thing. You can pray for them, but there won't be any impact.

Operating in deliverance comes with the wisdom, knowledge, and strategies of God himself. Every time the Lord called me to pray, he would tell me what part of my house he wanted me to pray in and what position he wanted me to be in. He specified the length of time he wanted me to pray—when to start and stop. It was very important to follow his orders.

One day, he told me to go into my son's room, get on my knees, and put my face on the floor. He was specific. He told me not to get up or lift my head until he was done. I did as I was told.

I began to pray, and as I was doing so, the Lord began to move. After I had prayed for about fifteen minutes, I felt the presence of spirits surrounding me. As I went to lift up my head, the Lord said, "Don't move!" So I stayed in position without lifting my head.

I pause from praying for a minute. I just wanted to know what was surrounding me. Then, all of a sudden, my mind was being tormented by what was around me. As I was praying, I could feel another set of spirits enter the room. When they did, the spirits that were surrounding me backed up. Then immediately, the spirits showed up a second time, surrounding me.

Still with my head down, I could see the Lord's angels fighting off the set of spirits that had me surrounded. I could see the Lord's angels holding hands in a circle. The demons that were trying to torment me were very angry. They were trying to reach past the Lord's angels to get to me. They were trying with everything they had to reach over the angels of God. They were fighting hard, but they were unsuccessful.

The fight went on until the Lord was done doing what he had to do for this pastor. *Wow!* I thought to myself. *We just don't know how we are protected in the spirit.*

I tell you, this assignment was crucial. "The effectual fervent prayer of a righteous man availeth much!" (James 5:16). Each assignment God gives us and the deeper he leads us into prayer will only bring us closer to him. What I had to learn is that he can call us into prayer at any time, so it's very important to stay connected to him in prayer.

One day while I was home doing household chores, all of a sudden, the Lord called out the name of one of my sons. I stopped what I was doing and said, "Lord, what is going on with my son?"

His response was, "Get your prayer shawl."

The way he said it to me, I knew it was trouble. So I ran into my bedroom, grabbed my shawl, and walked quickly into the living room.

The Lord said, "Kneel on the left side of your living room sofa!"

I was worried, not knowing what was going on with my son. I ran to the end of the sofa and kneeled before the Lord.

He said, "Trouble!" and took me into prayer.

I immediately saw my son walking by himself down the street. As I watched him walking, and as I prayed, the Lord said to my son, "Walk down this block and make a right turn!"

I saw my son make the right turn, although he had no idea what the Lord and I were doing back at the house. The Lord was commanding his spirit to do exactly as he was told.

After the turn, I saw my son was walking down a block where no one was. I prayed the blood of Jesus over him and commanded the spirit of death and murder off of his life.

Then I saw a white car with two guys driving around looking for my son to kill him. I saw them clearly as I continued to pray. The prayer lasted for a good fifteen to twenty minutes. Afterward, of course, as a mom, I was still shaken up with what the Lord had shown me. But I trusted God enough to know that the plans of the enemy for my son's life on that day were canceled.

I got up off the floor and put my prayer shawl back in my bedroom. I decided to take a walk to the store. As I was walking back from the store toward the house, I saw a white car driving slowly in my direction. As the car got closer, I looked at the guys in the car, and sure enough, they were the same guys the Lord had showed me thirty minutes earlier when I was in prayer.

The car had black tinted windows. The driver had the window down just enough to see out of it as he circled the blocks looking for my son. I looked at him with a smirk on my face, saying to myself, *Ha ha, devil, you lost again!* The Lord confused the enemy, and my son came home safe and sound.

Chapter 9

Anyone can go to the Lord in prayer. We can all make our requests known to him, and he will hear our prayers. But are our prayers answered? What is the Lord's response to our prayers? Are we coming out of prayer and seeing the results of what we are asking for? There are so many questions as to why some of our prayers are not answered.

As I mentioned, I was called into prayer for a certain pastor. Before the Lord allowed me to take on that assignment and go into prayer, he had to deal with me concerning something that I was still tied to.

It doesn't matter who you are or what title you hold—there are things you must get delivered and separate yourself from before you take on an assignment, especially when you're called by the Lord to do it. It cannot go into the

Lord's presence with you. There will be a block to what you're aiming for. You will be wasting precious prayer time.

But when the Lord calls the righteous, their prayers hit the bull's-eye. We can and will tear down every stronghold of the enemy when the Lord is leading us. The enemy knows what we are carrying. He watches and examines us diligently. If the enemy can identify within us anything that is attached to him, we are not a real threat to him in prayer.

Prayer is a sacred place that should not be taken lightly, especially if we want and have the heart to see people delivered. Operating in deliverance is not just going into prayer and asking the Lord to change a person. It becomes personal. There are so many things we need to carry into prayer while we are operating in deliverance.

God can and will use us, but are we willing and ready to sacrifice some things just to see others set free? There is a price to pay and also a great sacrifice. Are you ready to be used?

After we say *yes* to the Lord and accept the assignment he has given us, he will give us instructions of what to do, what to say, how to pray, and when to pray. Our obedience to God will bring great success in prayer—and our disobedience will cost us a whole lot.

Following the instructions of the Lord is extremely important. We must dot every *i* and cross every *t*. If we do not follow basic instructions, there will be no victory. Our victory is in our obedience.

For example, as I was on assignment for the pastor that I was praying for, I can remember the Lord saying to me, "Go into your son's room and kneel on the floor with your head down and don't stop praying until I tell you to." I did what he told me to do, and as I was praying, all of a sudden, there was a great attack by the enemy. I wanted to get up, but the Lord said, "Stay down!"

If I had not listened to the Lord and had gotten up and out of my position, I would have had to do that prayer all over again. So I said to myself, *No way!* The attack was too great, and I didn't want to stop and repeat my assignment. As bad as I wanted to get up, I stayed there and obeyed the Lord.

While I was praying with my face on the floor, the attack became extremely strong. The enemy tried so hard to stop me, but I continued to pray. All of a sudden, I heard a familiar voice. It was a well-known pastor who operated in deliverance. She wasn't there physically with me, but I heard her voice clearly in the spirit. She said to me, "Keep going, baby. You're almost done. They won't be able to get you the way they used too!"

It was as if she was in the room with me. I could hear her voice so loud and clear in my ear, as if she was standing right next to me. What she said helped me a lot. I was encouraged as she pushed me through the prayer. I found strength in my time of need.

There was a prayer chain going on, and it was powerful. As this well-known pastor obeyed God at that moment and took on the assignment to pray for me and encourage me to keep going, I was on assignment to pray for another pastor's deliverance. I was so glad for her obedience, because at that set time, I needed her. Thank God we were successful in prayer, and the devil lost the battle.

So this is why it's so important to obey the Lord when he calls us into prayer. Someone's life just may be depending on it! No matter what or how we may feel, we all must learn to obey the voice of God at all times. Our righteousness, prayers, and obedience can and will save lives.

This walk with the Lord has taught me that if we walk upright, as God commands us, it will benefit us all in a great way. As we enter into his presence, our minds, hearts, and spirits should be up to his standards. There will always be a blockage when unclean things are connected to us. We all should want our prayers to not only be heard but be effective and make a great impact at all times.

Prayer is a place of healing, deliverance, worship, and giving honor to God—a place where we can sabotage and cancel every plot and scheme of the enemy on our lives and the lives of our family members and friends. Fasting and praying are very powerful tools. When used together, we are walking in power.

The enemy doesn't know what to do with a person who has a daily prayer and fasting life. We are considered walking time bombs, fully loaded. We are a threat to his kingdom. This is why the enemy fights us so hard when we choose to obey the Lord with fasting and praying. He knows what a great impact and effect we would have on him his kingdom.

While I was on assignment for this particular pastor, the Lord put me on a concentration diet. It was very strict and hard. I was not allowed to consume any sweets, soda, or fried foods. I had never gone on fast like this one before. The Lord told me what to eat and when to eat it. Every day was different. Some days he wouldn't allow me to eat or drink anything at all.

One night, I was so hungry, I literally begged God to let me eat something and to have a glass of water! The day before, I had eaten nothing. With the intent of the prayers and the warfare, I became extremely hungry some days. This particular night, I felt like I hadn't eaten in days. I had tears in my eyes, so he decided to let me eat something.

I put enough food on my plate to last me until the next day. I was so happy, saying to myself, *I can finally eat!* But the Lord said to me, "Put a portion of the food back!"

I said, "Lord, please!"

He said, "Obey me!"

So I put a portion back in the pot.

I remember one night, I was in the middle of eating dinner when the Lord said to me, "Okay, put the food away!"

Although I was still hungry, I had to obey him.

There were some days where he wouldn't allow me to eat at all—not even a sip of water! My weight went down extremely quickly. I dropped three pants sizes.

Giving your yes to God will cost you something. I was on the fast for about a year, but it was worth it all.

A few years ago, I got a call in the middle of the night from someone asking me to pray for his friend's mother. The friend was with him when he made the call to me, and he put this friend on the phone to talk to me.

The friend said to me in an urgent voice, "My mother is in the hospital with internal bleeding, and the doctors are unable to stop the bleeding." He asked me if I could pray for her.

I said, "Sure I will." As I hung up the phone, I got out of bed and made a call to one of my prayer partners to pray with me concerning this woman with the issue of blood.

After my prayer partner and I finished praying, I began

to go back to bed, but the Lord said to me, "Continue to pray, but this time, pray alone!" So I did what the Lord asked me to do and continued to pray. My heart really went out to this woman. I had never met her, but my heart was filled with grief for her and the condition she was in.

While I was in prayer, the Lord decided to do something different. While I had been on the phone with my prayer partner, we had prayed for her, and there was nothing out of the ordinary. But when I went into prayer alone, the Lord said to me, while I was on my knees, "Stretch out your hand as if you were laying your hands on the woman, and command healing to her body!"

The Lord led me into prayer as if I was standing by her bedside. As I continued to pray for this woman, the Lord put me on an assignment for her. I just couldn't get this woman off my mind. I wanted the Lord to heal her. I mean, I picked up this woman's burdens for real.

About a week later, I got another phone call that her family had decided to prepare for the worst. They began to make funeral arrangements for her—they had no hope for her survival at all. It was as if she was already dead. All they had was what the doctors told them: that she had lost too much blood and there was nothing further that could be done to stop the bleeding. The doctors had no solution. They were unsure of how the bleeding started or how to stop it.

After hearing that, I got upset. I prayed even longer and harder. I believed that the Lord would heal her. As I continued to pray, I remembered what the Lord had said to me the very first night I prayed for her, and that was to stretch out my hand as if I was laying my hand on her body. I prayed and believed God with all of my heart.

At this point, I decided that I would go to the hospital to visit her. I just wanted to see her face-to-face so I could pray for her in person. Once I got to the hospital, however, I was unable to see her for various reasons. This woman was on my mind, and my heart was heavy.

One day at home, I was watching a Christian television program where there was a famous preacher praying for people. He had his hands stretched out toward the television as he prayed for those with all kinds of illness. As I sat there watching him pray, all of a sudden he said, "There's someone out there praying for a woman with internal bleeding!" He added, "The Lord is going to heal her!"

I was in shock at what he'd said. I jumped up from where I was sitting and begin to praise God and giving him things for her life. About a week later, I got word that she was being discharged from the hospital and was on her way home. The bleeding had stopped, and the funeral arrangements were canceled.

I was so excited. I really wanted to see who this woman was that the Lord had put on my heart to pray for. Most importantly, I wanted to let her know that it was the Lord who healed her—not the doctors or the medication, but the Lord himself.

Well, the Lord set it up where I was able to meet her over the phone. As we talked, I let her know that it was only the Lord that healed her. The Lord also put it in my heart to tell her how he'd allowed me to pray for her with my hands stretched out. I went on to tell her what the Lord wanted me to tell her. He said, "Let her know that she didn't realize how close she was to death and how bad her condition was."

She was in shock at what I told her. She began to tell me

that she knew that it was the Lord who healed her. She said, "I know the Lord, but I am a backslider."

She went on to tell me that she saw one of her girlfriends at the hospital one day, and this girlfriend stood by her bedside and began to pray for her. For some strange reason, she felt as if someone had laid hands on her. She looked up at her girlfriend, but her girlfriend was not touching her at all. She explained to her girlfriend what she'd felt, and the girlfriend said, "There was someone praying for you!"

The Lord also wanted me to tell her that she didn't just get healed, but it was a miracle. This woman was totally in shock about the things I told her and what the Lord had done for her. The greatest thing about this testimony was that this woman gave her life back to the Lord. She said that she was so grateful for what the Lord had done for her.

In the last book I wrote, *The Lord Rescued Me*, the Lord spoke to me about hospitals, doctors, and medications. He said there was a time coming when doctors wouldn't know what to do and medications wouldn't work. There would only be the Lord's healing power to rescue people out of their situations.

We the people of God must be prepared for that. A time is coming when the Lord will show his power and who he is on the earth. Many will return to the Lord. The churches will be packed. Many will come to the church looking for healing and to demonstrate the power of God and who he is. This will require us, the people of God, to be ready.

When the Lord led me to pray for the woman with the issue of blood, the doctors had no cure for her issue, nor did they have the knowledge of why it started or how to stop it. It was the Lord's power that healed her internal bleeding and kept her spirit from death.

This is why it's so important for us as God believers, intercessors, and prayer warriors to stay on the wall and keep ourselves connected to God through faithfulness and obedience. The Lord wants to get the glory on the earth and in the lives of people. Many people have been depending on their doctors and their medications for healing, but the Lord wants and will get the glory on the earth.

The Lord is not a respecter of persons. His healing power and deliverance are not just for believers. They're for anyone and everyone who will receive them. This is why we, the people of God, should never be in the mindset to judge anyone who is in a particular situation, especially the nonbelievers. Remember, we were not born saved. It was by God's grace that we all live through him. We should never have a heart to downgrade or to pick and choose who the Lord wants us to help. It is not our decision.

The Lord never looks down on anyone. As a matter of a fact, he sacrificed his life for all mankind. Prime example: when he was crucified on the cross, it wasn't just for the believers. The unbelievers were on his mind and heart as well. So who are we, the believers, to look down on, turn away, or judge anyone when it's the Lord's desire and good pleasure to bring the world out of these situations?

The heart of God is what's needed. Many hearts have waxed cold. I have seen many who are just themselves. They have no compassion for others. Let's go back to the old-time way, where we are not impressed with how packed our church services are, how big our megachurch buildings are, how much money our churches have, and how many private planes we have at our disposal, but how we look and sound when delivering the word of God. Trust me, all of that stuff does not impress the Lord, especially when it comes down to his work.

Don't get me wrong: the Lord wants to bless us. But that should never be our first priority, to the point where the Lord is no longer in it. We are losing ourselves and the passion and desire to see people set free from their issues. Our hearts should always be at a place where we are willing to join hands with the Lord to help bring someone out of their situation. If we are not doing this, what purpose are we serving?

It's time that we, the people of God, return to the Lord with all of our hearts and minds. The world is waiting on us!

About the Author

Natasha Cato is the author of *The Lord Rescued Me!* and *The Pain from Her Womb.* She's also the producer of the movie *The Pain from Her Womb.* She's a freelance writer and the owner of Kingdom Kidz Academy children's day care.

Tasha was born and raised in the Bedford Stuyvesant section of Brooklyn, New York, in a project called Eleanor Roosevelt Housing, where she lived for twenty-two years. She was raised on the rough streets of Do-or-Die Bed Stuy, and that is where this book's story begins.

Tasha's grandmother, the late Willie Mae Cato, wanted only the best for her. Mother Cato introduced Tasha to the church as a baby. However, the streets had a different plan for Tasha's life. She became a backslider and left the church.

At the age of seventeen, Tasha gave birth to her first son out of four boys, Nashawn Cato, while still under her grandmother's care. Mother Cato never gave up on her granddaughter as she continued to minister to and pray for her, constantly reminding her to never forget about God.

Tasha left home and started her own family. Her life took a major turn, but the Lord rescued her.

The National Domestic Violence Hotline

offers confidential one-on-one support twenty-four hours a day!

1800-799- SAFE (7233)
P.O. Box 161810
Austin, Texas 78716
Office line
512-453-8117

Made in the USA
Columbia, SC
30 March 2021

35273475R00045